More Great Piano Classics

Twenty-five world-famous pieces

Kevin Mayhew

We hope you enjoy *More Great Piano Classics*.
Further copies are available from your local music shop.

In case of difficulty, please contact the publisher direct:

The Sales Department
KEVIN MAYHEW LTD
Rattlesden
Bury St Edmunds
Suffolk IP30 0SZ

Phone 01449 737978
Fax 01449 737834

Please ask for our complete catalogue of outstanding Instrumental Music.

Front Cover: *Romantic Roses* by Eugène Henri Cauchois (1850-1911).
Reproduced by kind permission of Gavin Graham Gallery/
Fine Art Photographic Library, London.

Cover designed by Graham Johnstone
Picture Research: Veronica Ward

First published in Great Britain in 1995 by Kevin Mayhew Ltd

© Copyright 1995 Kevin Mayhew Ltd

ISBN 0 86209 667 7
Catalogue No: 3611157

Printed and bound in Great Britain

Contents

BARCAROLLE

Felix Mendelssohn (1809-1847)

PRELUDE

Maurice Ravel (1875-1937)

RONDO from Sonata K. 545

Wolfgang Amadeus Mozart (1756-1791)

POEM

Zdeněk Fibich (1850-1900)

PROMENADE from 'Pictures at an Exhibition'

Modest Musorgsky (1839-1881)

ÉCOSSAISE

Ludwig van Beethoven (1770-1827)

Fine

D.C. al Fine

WOODLAND FLOWERS

Robert Schumann (1810-1856)

GYMNOPÉDIE II

Erik Satie

21

BOURRÉE

Ludwig van Beethoven (1770-1827)

23

PRELUDE IN C MINOR

Frédéric Chopin (1810-1849)

SHEHERAZADE

Robert Schumann (1810-1856)

ADAGIO from Sonata K. 570

Wolfgang Amadeus Mozart (1756-1791)

ADAGIO from Sonata K. 570

Wolfgang Amadeus Mozart (1756-1791)

ALLEGRETTO

Felix Mendelssohn (1809-1847)

ANDANTE IN B♭

Wolfgang Amadeus Mozart (1756-1791)

NEW YEAR'S SONG

Robert Schumann (1810-1856)

CANTABILE

Frédéric Chopin (1810-1849)

ELEGY

Robert Schumann (1810-1856)

DEATH OF ASE

Edvard Grieg (1843-1907)

ANDANTE

Ludwig van Beethoven (1770-1827)

47

ALLA TURCA from Sonata K.331

Wolfgang Amadeus Mozart (1756-1791)

ROMANCE

Felix Mendelssohn (1809-1847)

ALLEGRETTO from 'Moonlight Sonata'

Ludwig van Beethoven (1770-1827)

Fine

D.C. al Fine

ANDANTE CON MOTO

Felix Mendelssohn (1809-1847)

BAGATELLE IN G MINOR

Ludwig van Beethoven (1770-1827)

62

WALTZ IN A

Franz Schubert (1797-1828)

P.B. 14
1702